MILITARY SERVICE

CAREERS IN THE
U.S. NAVY

MILITARY SERVICE

CAREERS IN THE
U.S. NAVY

BY EDWARD F. DOLAN

Marshall Cavendish
Benchmark
New York

Special thanks to CDR Stephen P. Trainor, military professor in the department of leadership, ethics, and law at the U.S. Naval Academy, for his review of the manuscript.

MARSHALL CAVENDISH BENCHMARK
99 WHITE PLAINS ROAD
TARRYTOWN, NY 10591
www.marshallcavendish.us

Copyright © 2010 by Marshall Cavendish Corporation

All rights reserved. No part of this book may be reproduced or utilized in any form or by any means electronic or mechanical, including photocopying, recording, or by any information storage and retrieval system, without permission from the copyright holders.

All Internet sites were available and accurate when this book was sent to press.

Library of Congress Cataloging-in-Publication Data
Dolan, Edward F., 1924–
Careers in the U.S. Navy / by Edward F. Dolan.
p. cm. — (Military service)
Includes bibliographical references and index.
Summary: "Discusses service in the U.S. Navy, including training, educational benefits, and career opportunities"—Provided by publisher.
ISBN 978-0-7614-4210-3
1. United States. Navy—Vocational guidance—Juvenile literature. I. Title.
VB259.D65 2008
359.0023'73—dc22
2008035919

EDITOR: Megan Comerford   PUBLISHER: Michelle Bisson
ART DIRECTOR: Anahid Hamparian   SERIES DESIGNER: Kristen Branch / Michael Nelson Design

Photo research by Candlepants Incorporated
Cover photo: Mass Communication Specialist Seaman Kyle D. Gahlau / U.S. Navy Photo
The photographs in this book are used by permission and through the courtesy of: *U.S. Navy Photo*: Mass Communication Specialist 3rd Class David Danals, 2,3; Mass Communication Specialist 3rd Class Michael A. Lantron, 7; Photographer's Mate 3rd Class Travis Ross, 10,11,back cover; Photographer's Mate Airman Brad Garner, 12,13; Mass Communication Specialist 2nd Class Zachary L. Borden, 16,17; Mr. Paul Farley, 22,23; Mass Communication Specialist 2nd Class Aaron Burden, 27; Chief Photographer's Mate Johnny Bivera, 30,31,73; Seaman Kevin T. Murray Jr., 33; Mass Communication Specialist 2nd Class Demetrius Kennon, 36; Chief Mass Communication Specialist Lucy M. Quinn, 38; Mass Communication Specialist Seaman Matt Daniels, 41; Journalist 2nd Class Brian P. Biller, 42,43; Photographer's Mate 1st Class Michael Worner, 45; Photographer's Mate 2nd Class Joseph C. Garza, 47; Mass Communication Specialist Seaman Joshua Martin, 49; Mass Communication Specialist 1st Class Chad J. McNeeley, 51; Chief Photographer's Mate Chris Desmond, 52,53; Gin Kai, 56; Mass Communication Specialist 2nd Class Katie Earley, 58; Photographer's Mate 2nd Class Eric S. Logsdon, 60; Mass Communication Specialist 3rd Class Kelly E. Barnes, 63; Mass Communication Specialist 3rd Class Kenneth R. Hendrix, 68,69; Chief Photographer's Mate Chris Desmond, 71. *Collection of the United States Senate*: 21. *U.S.Marine Corps Photo*: Staff Sgt. Jim Goodwin, 74.

Printed in Malaysia
1 3 5 6 4 2

CONTENTS

INTRODUCTION
THE BIRTH OF A NAVY — 6

ONE
AT SEA AND IN THE AIR — 12

TWO
JOBS IN THE NAVY — 30

THREE
PATHWAYS TO NAVAL SERVICE — 42

FOUR
FROM ENLISTMENT TO ASSIGNMENT — 52

FIVE
SALARY AND BENEFITS — 68

ACRONYM GLOSSARY — 76
FURTHER INFORMATION — 77
INDEX — 78

INTRODUCTION

THE BIRTH OF A NAVY

In October 1775, when the American Revolution was just six months old, members of the Continental Congress met in Philadelphia, Pennsylvania, to create a fleet to defend the thirteen colonies. The Congress had already established the Continental army and named George Washington its commander in chief. Even though the Congress was still debating what the colonies were fighting for—some wanted independence, others only more freedom of action under the British crown—all members understood that achieving their ends against the world's greatest naval power would be impossible without some sort of navy of their own.

On October 13 the Congress authorized the construction of two warships and established a marine committee to oversee all naval affairs. Then, on October 30, plans for two additional warships were approved. Finally, on November 28, the Continental Congress formally established a Continental navy.

Sailors line the deck of the USS *O'Kane*, an *Arleigh Burke*–class destroyer. The ship is returning to the naval station in Pearl Harbor, Hawaii, after a seven-month deployment.

CAREERS IN THE U.S. NAVY

Earlier in November the Congress authorized the formation of a unit of marines—seagoing soldiers who would be stationed aboard warships for offensive and defensive purposes. This unit was the precursor of the U.S. Marine Corps.

The four warships commissioned by Congress were never built. Instead, many smaller vessels—brigs, sloops, schooners, and frigates—were acquired and adapted for military use. These small ships were highly effective in sinking or capturing British munitions ships, troop transports, and merchantmen. In addition, Congress activated many civilian ships by issuing letters of marque. A letter of marque gave a ship's captain the authority to capture enemy vessels and confiscate their cargo.

Despite excellent performance, the American fleet was no more than a thorn in the side of the Royal Navy. The critical factor in the naval war was the alliance with France in 1778. It is unlikely that the Revolution would have been won without the support of the French fleet.

The surrender of the British forces at Yorktown, Virginia, in October 1781 effectively brought the fighting to an end; the Treaty of Paris in 1783 formally concluded the conflict between Great Britain and the thirteen colonies.

With independence achieved, the Continental Congress disbanded the army and the navy. The army was soon reestablished and grew rapidly in the ensuing years, since the nation, as it spread westward, had a steady need for soldiers.

THE BIRTH OF A NAVY

The United States did not have a navy, however, until 1794. During the 1790s the need for an armed naval defense became clear. With Britain and France almost continuously at war, the young United States earned the wrath of both by refusing to cooperate with either. Both nations began to attack U.S. merchant ships, seizing their cargoes and taking their crews prisoner. Around the same time, the Barbary Pirates—a group of raiders from the Muslim countries of North Africa that had long required European ships to pay tribute for safe passage through their waters—began attacking American ships and taking their cargoes.

In order to protect itself, Congress ordered the construction of six frigates (warships) in 1794 and put the navy under the U.S. War Department. In 1798, Congress authorized the formation of the Department of the Navy, which became part of the U.S. Department of Defense in 1947.

With close to 300 ships and more than 3,700 aircraft, the U.S. Navy is one of the strongest and most modern naval forces in the world. As of 2009, its active-duty roster consisted of more than 380,000 officers and enlisted men and women. In addition, there were approximately 158,000 personnel on Reserve duty. Together, the two groups fill positions in more than sixty occupational fields that include aviation, nuclear propulsion, air traffic control, medicine, electronics, and ship-and-shore fire control.

This book is aimed primarily at young men and women who are thinking of joining the U.S. Navy. One reader may

CAREERS IN THE U.S. NAVY

THE BIRTH OF A NAVY

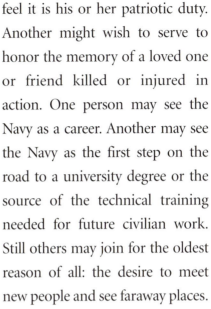

The USS *Theodore Roosevelt* receives personnel and logistics support from Sea Stallion helicopters.

feel it is his or her patriotic duty. Another might wish to serve to honor the memory of a loved one or friend killed or injured in action. One person may see the Navy as a career. Another may see the Navy as the first step on the road to a university degree or the source of the technical training needed for future civilian work. Still others may join for the oldest reason of all: the desire to meet new people and see faraway places.

Time spent in the Navy, no matter how long, brings rewards. It provides training and a sense of discipline that are useful in civilian life. The academic and practical experience that men and women receive in a variety of technical, administrative, and service areas are respected assets in both military and civilian careers. Former members of the military are increasingly sought by civilian employers.

The U.S. Navy has quite a lot to offer.

AT SEA AND IN THE AIR

IN THE U.S. NAVY, EVERY SAILOR AND officer belongs to one of two groups. The first is the Navy's combat forces; the second is the support services, which allow the combat personnel to do their jobs wherever they may be serving.

COMBAT FORCES

All of the U.S. Navy's ships and aircraft are assigned to one of three units: the combat surface forces, the submarine forces, or the naval air forces.

COMBAT SURFACE FORCES

There are five types of ships in the combat surface forces. They are aircraft carriers, amphibious assault ships, cruisers, destroyers, and frigates.

Members of the deck crew aboard the USS *Theodore Roosevelt* prepare the aircraft of Carrier Air Wing 1 for a mission in 2002. The color of each sailor's uniform indicates his or her job.

SHIPS IN THE NAVY

Ships are the centerpieces of the U.S. Navy. Two basic letter designations are used for all navy ships—USS and USNS. USS stands for "United States ship"; a ship so designated is a commissioned naval vessel and has the authority to act on behalf of the government. USNS stands for "United States naval ship" and refers to noncommissioned vessels manned by civilians employed by the Navy. These ships perform a variety of duties; some carry ammunition and oil, while others carry crews assigned to special jobs such as cable repair and acoustic surveys.

All USS ships are named by the secretary of the Navy. USS vessels are customarily named for states, cities, towns, animals, and important historical figures; some of the best known are the USS *Dwight D. Eisenhower* (aircraft carrier), the USS *Ticonderoga* (cruiser), and the USS *Wasp* (amphibious assault ship).

AIRCRAFT CARRIERS The aircraft carrier was first used in World War II and has become the twenty-first-century Navy's principal fighting ship. On a carrier, planes are housed, maintained, launched, and retrieved in attacks on enemy land, sea, and airborne targets. Through the years, carriers have been outfitted with increasingly advanced launching and retrieval systems. The launching system consists of steam-powered catapults that can fling a plane into the air along a 300-foot (91.4-m) path at a speed of 165 miles per hour (265.5 km/h) in 2 seconds. The retrieval system, which comes into play when a plane returns to the carrier, features four steel cables that lie flat on the deck. Each aircraft is fitted with a tailhook, extending from the aircraft's underside, that catches one of the steel cables, which is then yanked upward to make a fence extending the width of the deck.

AT SEA AND IN THE AIR

The plane, which is traveling at 150 mph (240 km/h), is pulled to a stop in some 320 feet (97.5 m).

In all, there are eleven vessels in the nation's carrier force, with a twelfth under construction for release in 2009. The flight deck of a carrier measures over 1,000 ft. (305 m) in length (nearly the length of three football fields). The superstructure—called the island—rises five decks above the flight deck; there are another seven decks below the flight deck, with the ship's engine room at the bottom. A carrier is classified as one of three classes, or types, depending on what specific characteristics it has. A class is named for the first ship of a given design.

1. KITTY HAWK CLASS. This class consists of a single carrier, the USS *Kitty Hawk*. The ship, which was launched in 1975, is 1,062.5 ft. (323.8 m) long and houses a propulsion system of eight boilers and four steam turbines that give it a speed of over 30 knots (55.6 km/h). (Speed at sea is measured in knots—nautical miles per hour. One nautical mile equals 1.15 standard miles.) It carries a ship crew of 3,150 officers and sailors, and an air wing of 2,480. The sailors in the air wing, which has its own officers and chain of command, maintain and fly the carrier's eighty-five planes.

2. ENTERPRISE CLASS. The USS *Enterprise* is the only vessel in this class. Launched in 1960, the ship was the nation's first nuclear propulsion aircraft carrier. It is 1,101 ft. (335.6 m) long, has a propulsion system that consists of eight nuclear

CAREERS IN THE U.S. NAVY

reactors, and can travel at speeds of more than 30 knots (55.6 km/h). The ship's regular crew and air wing total 5,830, and it has eighty-five aircraft.

3. *NIMITZ* CLASS. The *Nimitz* class includes nine ships, with a tenth (the USS *George H. W. Bush*) scheduled to enter service in 2009. The ships in this class are the largest warships in the world. *Nimitz* carriers run to lengths of 1,092 ft. (332.85 m). They are powered by two nuclear reactors and are capable of speeds exceeding 30 knots (55.6 km/h). Each ship in the *Nimitz* class carries regular crews of 3,200, an air wing of 2,480, and eighty-five aircraft.

The USS *George H. W. Bush* will include several cutting-edge technological features, such as new radar towers, an upgraded navigational system, and a new aircraft launching and recovery system. This is the final ship in the *Nimitz* class. It will be replaced by the *Gerald R. Ford* class, the first of which is under construction and scheduled for delivery to the Navy in 2015.

AT SEA AND IN THE AIR

The USS *Wasp* is a multipurpose amphibious assault ship. It carries a naval crew as well as a detachment of marines. The MV-22 Ospreys lined up on the deck are being prepped for a mission in the Middle East during the War on Terrorism. The medical facilities onboard can accommodate 600 casualties.

CAREERS IN THE U.S. NAVY

AMPHIBIOUS ASSAULT SHIPS U.S. amphibious ships have long been known by the nickname Gator Navy because, like alligators, these vessels can travel very quickly in water. The amphibious assault ship is the main type of land-and-water–capable ship in the U.S. Navy, which has the largest amphibious force in the world.

Amphibious assault ships are smaller than aircraft carriers and only carry tilt-rotor and rotary-wing planes, both of which are capable of vertical or short takeoffs and landings (V/STOL, STOVL, VTOL). These ships and their aircraft transport and retrieve Marine combat units. U.S. amphibious assault ships, which are the largest assault ships in the world, are able to sail swiftly into enemy fire and put troops ashore by means of helicopter or landing craft.

In the U.S. Navy amphibious ships are divided into the *Wasp* class and the *Tarawa* class. There is a third class still in the design stage and scheduled to go on duty in 2013.

1. *Wasp* CLASS. The *Wasp*-class ship is powered by two geared steam turbines and two gas turbines. The vessels in this class measure 844 ft. (253.5 m) long and are capable of speeds in excess of 20 knots (37 km/h). All seven ships in the class carry a crew of 900 to 1,100 sailors and officers and a detachment of approximately 1,900 Marines; there is an eighth ship scheduled for completion in 2009.
2. *Tarawa* CLASS. This class features steam-powered ships that measure 820 ft. (250 m) in length. Each of the three

AT SEA AND IN THE AIR

Tarawa-class ships is manned by a crew of 964 sailors and officers and a detachment of 1,900 marines. Ships in both the *Tarawa* and *Wasp* classes carry twenty-nine aircraft: usually twelve Sea Knight, four Sea Stallion, three Huey, and four Super Cobra helicopters, and six Harrier attack aircraft.

The Gator Navy also includes amphibious transport docks; each dock is effectively a flight deck with a well that can be filled with water to stabilize it to make boarding or embarking landing craft easier. There are also dock landing ships designed to serve as transport for air-cushion vessels, conventional landing craft, and helicopters.

CRUISERS Cruisers are large warships that support aircraft carriers and amphibious forces in battle and perform various other missions. Throughout their long history in naval warfare, they have been known by a variety of names: battle cruisers, armored cruisers, and heavy and light cruisers.

The cruiser's principal weapon is the missile; many cruisers are equipped with a weapons system whose radar can track up to one hundred targets at once. Most cruisers are also outfitted with vertical launch systems (VLS) for long-range precision Tomahawk missiles.

Cruisers measure 567 ft. (172.8 m) in length and are powered by four gas turbine engines. Each carries four helicopters: two Seasprites and two Sea Hawks. All cruisers, which are *Ticonderoga*-class ships, have crews of 364 sailors and officers. The USS *Ticonderoga*, which was retired from service in 2004, and the other twenty-two cruisers are named after memorable battle sites.

DESTROYERS   Modern destroyers are divided into two categories—conventional destroyers and guided missile destroyers. Both types protect and support carrier groups in battle, along with other surface vessels and amphibious units. Conventional destroyers perform antisubmarine duty; guided missile destroyers engage in air, surface, and submarine warfare. Their main weapons are the Harpoon anti-ship cruise missile and the Tomahawk missile.

Destroyers are classified in the *Arleigh Burke* class, which is named for the Navy's most famous World War II destroyer commander and three-time chief of naval operations. Each destroyer is powered by four gas turbines and has a 323-member crew. In all, there are fifty-seven ships in the class, but only the twenty newest ships are equipped with missiles. Many destroyers are named for prominent historical—usually naval—figures, including the *John Paul Jones* and *John S. McCain*.

FRIGATES   A frigate is a modern warship that is smaller than a destroyer. Frigates serve mainly as antisubmarine vessels but also engage in a number of other combat duties, such as landing amphibious forces and protecting arriving merchant convoys. Each vessel is equipped with two gas turbine engines,

"I HAVE NOT YET BEGUN TO FIGHT!"

John Paul Jones was America's first naval hero. His ship, the *Bonhomme Richard*, was an aging vessel acquired from the French after the 1778 alliance. In the summer of 1779, Jones was in command of several ships attacking British merchant vessels sailing out of ports along the English Channel. On September 23, 1779, Jones sighted a convoy of merchantmen under the protective escort of two warships, the *Serapis* and the *Countess of Scarborough*.

Jones immediately engaged the *Serapis*. Within minutes both vessels were in flames and firing upon each other at point-blank range. The ships collided, but sailors proceeded to engage in hand-to-hand combat. Fighting continued through the evening as fire gutted the two ships. When a British shell pierced one of the *Richard*'s water pumps, the American crew feared they were sinking. The captain of the *Serapis*, hearing the commotion, asked Jones if he was surrendering. Jones's proud and defiant answer has been immortalized: "I have not yet begun to fight!"

It seemed that the *Serapis* was soon to be the victor until Jones was able to maneuver his ship alongside the *Serapis* and unleash a barrage along its length. The British captain, recognizing that his ship was going down, lowered the flag. Jones and his crew boarded the *Serapis*, accepted its surrender, and sailed to a nearby French port. The battle was not only the first victory of an American warship, but also the final naval battle of the Revolutionary War. The remainder of the war was fought on land and concluded with the American victory at Yorktown, Virginia, in 1781.

Above: John Paul Jones secured the first American victory over a British warship during the Revolutionary War. There is a destroyer named after him.

CAREERS IN THE U.S. NAVY

reaches speeds of 29 knots (53.7 km/h), and is manned by 194 sailors and officers. On board are Harpoon missiles, torpedoes, and two aircraft. The ships are listed as *Oliver Hazard Perry*–class vessels. The first in the class, which is named for the American naval hero of the War of 1812, was retired from service in 1997. As of 2009, there were thirty ships in service.

AT SEA AND IN THE AIR

The hull of the USS *Montpelier*, a *Los Angeles*–class attack submarine, surfaces off the coast Crete, Greece. The sub is part of the Harry S. Truman carrier strike group, which is made up of seven U.S. naval vessels, one Canadian frigate, and one British destroyer.

SUBMARINE FORCES

The U.S. Navy has two different kinds of submarines: ballistic missile subs ("boomers") and attack subs ("boats").

BALLISTIC MISSILE SUBMARINES Ballistic missile subs belong to the *Ohio* class. They are easily recognized by their

CAREERS IN THE U.S. NAVY

fish-shaped hulls, which enable them to move through the water quietly at speeds of 20 knots (37 km/h) or faster. An *Ohio*-class submarine is 560 ft. (170.7 m) long and has a crew of 155 sailors and officers. These subs can remain beneath the surface for months at a time.

The primary mission of boomers is to discourage nuclear attack. They carry nuclear Trident missiles, guided Tomahawk missiles, and MK-48 torpedoes. Of the fourteen boats in the class, all but one are named for a state. The USS *Henry Jackson* is named for the longtime senator from the state of Washington who vigorously championed a strong military defense.

ATTACK SUBMARINES Attack submarines are craft that strike both surface and subsurface enemy vessels. In addition, boats have long served a wide variety of special purposes, including reconnaissance missions and the delivery and retrieval of commando forces. All modern submarines are equipped with nuclear reactors, attain speeds of 25 knots (46 km/h), and are armed with Tomahawk missiles for attack and MK-48 torpedoes for defense. There are three classes of attack subs.

1. LOS ANGELES CLASS. There are more *Los Angeles*–class boats on duty than in any other submarine class—fifty-one in all. These fast, heavily armed boats are designed primarily to destroy surface and subsurface enemy targets, but are also dispatched on intelligence-gathering missions. They each carry a crew of 134 sailors and officers. The U.S. Navy calls the *Los Angeles* class "the backbone" of its attack sub-

AT SEA AND IN THE AIR

marine force. The twenty-three most recent subs are designated Improved 688s (I688s) because they are quieter, have advanced combat systems, and can carry out operations under ice. All *Los Angeles*–class boats are named for American cities except the USS *Hyman G. Rickover*, which is named after the admiral who headed the navy's nuclear submarine development program from 1948 to 1972.

2. SEAWOLF CLASS. *Seawolf* submarines are designed to operate silently on and beneath the surface and may be the best armed of all submarines. Each measures 353 ft. (107.6 m) or 453 ft. (138 m) long and is manned by 140 sailors and officers.

3. VIRGINIA CLASS. This is the newest of the three classes of attack submarines. Five *Virginia*-class boats are already at sea, another is under construction, and three more are planned. *Virginia*-class boats carry crews of 134 enlisted sailors and officers. Each features a new design system that enables the control room and its periscope mount to be placed at a lower level in the boat than was previously possible. Like boats in the *Ohio* class, *Virginia*-class submarines are named for states.

Service aboard a submarine is recognized as one of the more demanding jobs in the Navy. Sailors assigned to submarine duty undergo intense physical and technical training at the U.S. Naval Submarine School in Groton, Connecticut, in preparation for their jobs. The physical training is done in three phases and is geared toward preparing submarine crews for the intense pressures endured in beneath-the-sea work.

CAREERS IN THE U.S. NAVY

NAVAL AIR FORCES

The naval air forces—consisting of U.S. Navy and Marine Corps units—are made up of sea-based and land-based aircraft. Sea-based aircraft are assigned to carriers and several smaller ships. Those aboard aircraft carriers serve in what are known as air wings. A wing includes several kinds of aircraft, such as fighters, weather ships, and helicopters. The planes stationed aboard a *Nimitz*-class ship are representative of those on all carriers and include Hornets, Hawkeyes, Prowlers, Super Hornets, Seahawk helicopters, and Greyhounds. The aircraft are divided into a number of categories; there is more than one type of plane in most categories.

1. FIGHTER OR ATTACK AIRCRAFT. The Hornet was the nation's first strike fighter and is designed to attack at night and in all weather conditions. This category also includes Super Hornets, Raptors, and Prowlers.

2. TRANSPORT AIRCRAFT. The Globemaster, known for its rapid troop and equipment deliveries, hauls cargoes of all weights and sizes to supply bases. This category also includes the Hercules, Skytrain, and Stratotanker in-flight refueler.

3. PATROL AIRCRAFT. The Orion is a long-range, antisubmarine warfare (ASW) aircraft fitted with advanced sensors that are integrated by computer. This category also includes the Multimission Maritime Aircraft (MMA).

4. EARLY-WARNING AIRCRAFT. The Hawkeye provides all-weather information and warnings for a carrier battle

AT SEA AND IN THE AIR

A fighter pilot in a Hornet awaits for an aircraft handler to signal him into launch position aboard the USS *Ronald Reagan*. His mask delivers breathable air while in flight, while the jumpsuit, called a "G-suit," protects his body from the gravitational forces incurred at high speeds. The pilot's helmet cushions his head, provides noise protection, and has radio equipment.

group. It also flies surface surveillance and search-and-rescue missions.

5. HELICOPTER. The Osprey is a tilt-rotor aircraft—it can take off vertically, quickly shift to horizontal flight, and return to vertical flight for landings. Among its duties are the delivery and retrieval of combat units and the transport of troops, including their supplies and equipment.

SUPPORT SERVICES

U.S. naval forces are divided into six fleets; the Second, Third, and Fourth are located in the U.S. while the Fifth, Sixth, and

CAREERS IN THE U.S. NAVY

Seventh are in Bahrain, Italy, and Japan, respectively. To serve all its ships and personnel, the navy maintains more than fifty bases of varying sizes in twenty states and Washington, DC, as well as approximately eighty worldwide.

The bases are responsible for a wide variety of services. Many serve as naval air stations and provide aircraft for sea and land duty and for training purposes. Others are bases for specific types of vessels, such as the amphibious base at Norfolk, Virginia, and the submarine base at Groton, Connecticut. Some bases provide specific services including the Naval Construction Battalion Center (NCBC) in Gulfport, Mississippi, and the Earle Naval Weapons Station in Colts Neck, New Jersey. The following bases rank among the largest.

NORFOLK, VIRGINIA. This amphibious-ship installation includes a naval shipyard and a naval air station, in addition to extensive port facilities. Covering over 4,600 acres (18.6 km^2), it is the world's largest operating naval base. The Second Fleet is stationed here.

SAN DIEGO, CALIFORNIA. This submarine installation consists of a cluster of bases and serves as the chief naval port on the West Coast. San Diego also serves as the base for the Third Fleet.

PEARL HARBOR, HAWAII. Since 1887, Pearl Harbor has served as a U.S. naval base and as the headquarters of the Pacific Fleet. It has operated a naval shipyard since 1908; its shops and dry docks are able to service all types of ships. In memory of the Japanese attack on December 7, 1941, during

AT SEA AND IN THE AIR

World War II, it is the site of the USS *Arizona* memorial.

KITSAP, WASHINGTON. This installation is the home base for *Ohio*-class submarines operating in the Pacific Ocean.

KINGS BAY, GEORGIA. This installation is the home base for *Ohio*-class submarines operating in the Atlantic Ocean.

PENSACOLA, FLORIDA. The naval air station here serves as a main base for training Navy and Marine Corps pilots.

THE PENTAGON, WASHINGTON, DC. Not strictly a base, this building houses the central administrative offices and all the component parts of the Department of Defense. One of the largest buildings in the world, the Pentagon occupies approximately 3.7 million square feet (411,111 m^2) of office space.

GUANTÁNAMO BAY, CUBA. This base, located on a section of Cuba's southeastern coast, was leased to the United States by the Cuban government in 1903, in the wake of the Spanish-American War. The lease cannot be ended unless both the U.S. and Cuban governments agree. Guantánamo Bay has been used since October 2001 as a detention center for suspected terrorists.

YOKOSUKO, JAPAN. Situated at the entrance to Tokyo Bay, the Yokosuko base is the largest of the Navy's overseas facilities. It has been an American installation since the Japanese surrender that ended World War II in 1945. Prior to that time, it had been a major Japanese naval installation. The Seventh Fleet is stationed at Yokosuko.

JOBS IN THE NAVY

THE NAVY REQUIRES THE SKILLS AND untiring dedication of men and women of all ranks and in all work areas in order to keep its ships, submarines, aircraft, and bases in the best operational order possible. The Navy has more than sixty different job fields, all of which can lead to successful careers. Some 800 jobs become available each week as personnel leave the service.

In the U.S. Navy and Coast Guard, the jobs that are open to enlisted personnel are called ratings; no degree is required. These jobs are known as military occupation specialties (MOS) in the Army and the Marine Corps and as specialty codes in the Air Force. There are also jobs available to officers with degrees in subjects such

Navigation is an important skill for any sailor. During a battle stations drill aboard the USS *Vella Gulf*, a guided-missile cruiser, Quartermaster 1st Class William Pomeroy plots the ship's course. The sailor is wearing flash gear for fire protection and a gas mask as part of the drill.

CAREERS IN THE U.S. NAVY

as law and engineering, and health-care positions for men and women who have earned medical degrees.

RATINGS

The ratings for enlisted naval personnel are divided into twenty-nine major categories.

ADMINISTRATION RATINGS

A wide variety of administrative positions are available both aboard ships and ashore. Administration workers are responsible for updating and keeping accurate records of a unit's personnel, equipment, and supplies. Jobs include dispersing clerk, data processing technician, and storekeeper. Administrative careers for enlisted personnel are available in fields such as business management, legal administration, office and administrative support, purchasing and supply, and finance and accounting; assignment is often based on aptitude.

AVIATION

Sailors in the aviation field work on both air and ground crews to provide vital attack, defense, and logistic support to the Navy's air fleet. The most recognizable are the aircraft carrier pilots and the deck personnel, who supervise the launching and retrieval of planes. Both enlisted sailors and officers serve on deck crews. They wear brightly colored uniforms that indicate their jobs. For example, aviation fuel handlers wear purple; aircraft handling officers, catapult and

JOBS IN THE NAVY

Two members of the deck crew on board the USS *Harry S. Truman* wait for a final signal before giving the pilot the go-ahead to launch. The Navy compares launch preparations to a well-choreographed ballet.

arresting gear officers, and plane directors wear yellow; and ordnance men, crash and salvage crews, and explosive ordnance disposal crews wear red. Other jobs include air traffic controller, aviation structural mechanic, aviation antisubmarine operator, and electronic warfare technician.

CONSTRUCTION AND BUILDING

Construction workers build and repair every type of structure needed by the Navy, including shipboard plumbing and piping systems, living quarters, warehouses, docks, and airfields. Within the field there are many areas of specialization,

CAREERS IN THE U.S. NAVY

such as carpentry and electrical work. Jobs include builder, utilities worker, and hull maintenance technician.

EDUCATION

Members of the educational community teach and mentor Navy personnel in everything from marksmanship to operating aircrew survival gear. Sailors in this occupational specialty oversee the advancement of junior personnel, provide hands-on instruction, and are responsible for career counseling.

ELECTRONICS AND COMPUTERS

Workers in these fields are responsible for the installation, maintenance, and repair of the sophisticated electrical equipment and electronic and computer systems. Electronics workers encode and decode ship-to-ship communications, test generators and motors, and work with aviation and missile-launching systems. Sailors who specialize in computers evaluate intercepted radar signals, operate underwater communications systems, and track targets, among other duties.

EMERGENCY, FIRE, AND RESCUE, AND LAW ENFORCEMENT AND SECURITY

Sailors in these categories serve as firefighters, emergency medical technicians, and security personnel. Those in the emergency, fire, and rescue field maintain shipboard damage control and work to prevent emergency situations; they are trained to provide assistance when accidents do happen. The law enforce-

JOBS IN THE NAVY

ment and security field employs sailors that train narcotic- and bomb-detecting dogs, conduct crime prevention programs, and train others in shore-patrol duties.

FOOD, RESTAURANT, AND LODGING

Navy personnel in this field prepare meals for sailors and officers aboard ships and at shore stations, operate the galleys, and manage shipboard living quarters. Those with strong culinary skills may even prepare meals for foreign dignitaries or White House guests.

INTELLIGENCE AND COMMUNICATIONS

Intelligence and communications specialists collect, analyze, and communicate information on current and anticipated enemies, often using surveillance systems and radar. Sailors in this field work with a ship's Identification Friend or Foe (IFF) system, operate the Navy's global satellite telecommunications systems, and maintain combat information center (CIC) displays of tactical information.

MECHANICAL AND INDUSTRIAL

Work in this field entails the operation and maintenance of all the tools, equipment, and machinery associated with the ships, submarines, aircraft, and weapons systems utilized by the Navy. Sailors can specialize in navigation, communication, or transportation systems. Some mechanical and industrial workers become members of the Fighting Seabees, the Navy frontline

CAREERS IN THE U.S. NAVY

The nickname "Seabees" comes from CB, the abbreviation for construction battalion. There are five kinds of Seabee units: supervisory, mobile, amphibious, underwater, and shore. Each team has workers that specialize in different aspects of construction, such as steelworking or engineering. Here, members of the Naval Mobile Construction Battalion 1 pour concrete at the naval base in Guam.

construction battalion. The Seabees build the structures required for land-to-sea and sea-to-land movement for ships, aircraft, machinery, and personnel.

MEDIA AND PUBLIC AFFAIRS RATINGS

Enlisted Navy personnel can work in fields such as music, information technology, news and media, telecommunications, and world languages. The Navy has many different bands that perform at special events and in parades; instrumentalists and vocalists can work in the music field. Sailors skilled in high-tech work, such as with networks and integrated

JOBS IN THE NAVY

information systems, are needed in the information technology field. Those in the news and media field are expected to distribute visual, audio, and written information within the Navy itself and to the public; sailors can work as photographers, writers, or editors. Sailors working in telecommunications ratings maintain systems from communication to alarm and work with classified machinery coding. Since the U.S. Navy is a worldwide presence, it needs intelligent sailors fluent in foreign languages to translate, transcribe, and interpret communications, often classified material.

MEDICAL AND DENTAL

Health care ranks as one of the largest career fields in the Navy. Men and women in this field work aboard ships and at onshore installations, including large hospitals and small clinics, as Navy hospital corpsmen and dental technicians. Health care specialization is available in fields such as emergency treatment, radiology, and search and rescue. There are further opportunities in areas such as optometry or biochemistry for those who hold degrees of higher education.

RELIGION AND HUMAN RESOURCES

Men and women who work in these two fields are responsible for enhancing the morale of sailors and providing guidance. Those in the religion occupational specialty assist Navy chaplains in morally, spiritually, and emotionally supporting sailors and their families. Sailors working in human

WOMEN IN THE NAVY

American women have aided the military since the Revolutionary War. In 1778 Mary Ludwig Hays (nicknamed Molly Pitcher) carried water to the American troops fighting at the Battle of Monmouth. Women also served as nurses and laundry workers in the Revolutionary War and in the Civil War; a few even disguised themselves as men and fought as soldiers.

In World War I approximately 21,000 women served the Army and Navy as nurses, while another 13,000 worked as office personnel for the Navy and the Marine Corps. In World War II the number of women in uniform jumped to more than 350,000 throughout the armed forces. Most worked in the medical and administrative fields, though a number served as pilots (chiefly ferrying planes), truck drivers, mechanics, electricians, and gunnery instructors.

In 1942 the nation established a Navy Reserve program for women called Women Accepted for Voluntary Emergency Service, or WAVES. Along with the WAVES, sister groups in all the services were established: WAC (Women's Army Corps), SPARS (U.S. Coast Guard Women's Reserve), the U.S. Marine Corps Women Reserve, and WASP (Women Air Service Pilots).

During the war WAVES worked as storekeepers, office personnel, drivers, mechanics, cryptologists, parachute riggers, and air-traffic controllers. There were 86,000 WAVES by mid-1945.

The wartime work of women brought the realization in Washington that women should have a permanent place in the nation's military forces. In 1948 Congress passed the Women's Armed Services Integration Act. The measure codified the position of women in the military. Like men, they could hold regular military ranks and receive the privileges that came with rank. Limitations were placed on enlistment and promotion, however, and they were barred from combat duty.

In the next years women's role in the military grew. They served in Korea, Vietnam, the Persian Gulf, and Panama. Thanks to a number of court rulings, female officers won the right to command units composed of both men and women, the separate training of males and females came to an end, and the financial entitlements for dependents were made the same for both male and female service people.

In addition, positions that had once been limited to men were extended to women. In 1973 the first female pilots won their wings. Three years later, in 1976, the first female cadets were accepted by the U.S. Naval Academy at Annapolis, Maryland, and the term WAVES was discontinued. Then, two years later, though still banned from combat areas, women were allowed to serve at sea aboard noncombatant ships. Women are now free to hold any job in the Navy, with two exceptions. They are not permitted to serve with Navy SEALs (and similar units) or to serve aboard submarines.

Left: During Navy Week Detroit in 2007, LT Ladonna Gordon (left) and LT Kathryn S. Wijnaldum spoke to two high school seniors about Navy life. Every year the Navy hosts Navy Weeks across the country, often in cities without a significant Navy presence. The Navy aims to convey what the Navy does, why it is important, and the existing opportunities for young Americans.

CAREERS IN THE U.S. NAVY

resources provide career counseling to candidates; inform personnel of education, training, and promotion opportunities; and recruit young men and women to join the Navy.

SPECIAL OPERATIONS

The Navy has four special operations forces (SOF): the sea, air, land teams (SEALs), special warfare combatant-craft crewmen (SWCCs), explosive ordnance disposal technicians (EOD), and Navy divers. All four SOFs handle unconventional warfare operations that require stealth, skill, strength, and training. SEALs and SWCCs may conduct secret landings in enemy territory for reconnaissance and sabotage; EODs are often assigned to reconnaissance missions and the demolition of enemy installations; and Navy divers are called in for underwater salvage and demolition operations.

Members of naval SOFs must not only be in excellent physical condition, but they must also be motivated, disciplined, and able to perform under extreme pressure. Navy SEALs undergo what many consider to be the most physically and mentally demanding training in the military. In addition to normal military pay, SEALs receive a $40,000 enlistment bonus, which is the highest paid by the Navy.

TRANSPORTATION AND LOGISTICS

Workers in this field are in charge of safely and efficiently transporting troops, supplies, equipment, and machinery to destinations worldwide. Men and women working in

JOBS IN THE NAVY

Navy SEALs are air-dropped to secure a beach. To become a SEAL, a sailor must undergo a year-long initial training period, eighteen months of pre-deployment training, and intensive specialized training.

transportation and logistics use navigational and radar equipment, keep inventory and financial records, understand ocean currents, coordinate transport missions, and organize post offices and supply issue.

GETTING THE RIGHT JOB

Navy enlistees first learn about the job opportunities from a recruiter. After learning about the duties and responsibilities of each one, the enlistee chooses three that are especially appealing and that best match his or her personality, interests, and abilities. These choices may lead to more than just a job—they may lead to a career.

THREE

PATHWAYS
TO NAVAL SERVICE

THERE ARE FOUR WAYS TO SERVE IN THE U.S. Navy: by enlisting in the active-duty Navy, by joining the U.S. Navy Reserve or the Naval Reserve Officers Training Corps (NROTC), or as a graduate from the U.S. Naval Academy at Annapolis, Maryland. A naval academy graduate can join the Navy as an ensign or the Marine Corps as a second lieutenant. Everyone who dons the navy blue, however, must meet certain requirements.

- They must be a U.S. citizen or meet noncitizen requirements.
- They must be between the ages of seventeen and thirty-four; those who are seventeen need parental consent.
- They must be high school graduates or have a high school equivalency diploma.

Despite all the advanced communications systems available to Navy personnel, basic visual communications such as flashing light and semaphore (flag signals) are still important. Quartermaster 3rd Class Kearah Critchfield trains on the signal bridge of the USS *Harpers Ferry*, an amphibious dock landing ship, while stationed in the Philippines in 2006.

CAREERS IN THE U.S. NAVY

Enlistees must also pass urinalysis tests for drug and alcohol abuse and must meet a variety of legal and medical standards.

ON ACTIVE DUTY WITH THE NAVY

An active-duty sailor usually signs on for a four- to six-year tour of duty. As of 2009, there were more than 381,000 men and women in the active-duty force. Of that total, approximately 323,000 were enlisted sailors, 5,000 were midshipmen, and 53,000 were officers.

A sailor's career begins with the instructional period called boot camp. Similar training programs exist in all branches of the military. Boot camp, an introduction to Navy life, lasts eight weeks, and is usually followed by a period of schooling or on-the-job training in a specific field of work.

A sailor wishing to make the Navy a lifelong career may advance through the ranks; rank promotion is accompanied by an increase in responsibility as well as pay. Retirement is possible after twenty years of service. All naval careers are divided into periods of enlistment. At the close of each enlistment period, a sailor may leave the Navy, continue in service, or join a Reserve unit.

U.S. NAVY RESERVE

The U.S. Navy Reserve first formed in 1915, replacing the Naval Militia. The Naval Militia was composed of several state units—in essence, they were the seagoing equivalent of the Army National Guard. Like the National Guard, the militias

PATHWAYS TO NAVAL SERVICE

Navy recruits perform an "abandon ship" drill during boot camp at Great Lakes, Illinois. Recruits must jump into the water, buddy up, and successfully climb into the life raft.

CAREERS IN THE U.S. NAVY

were under state jurisdiction unless congressional action placed them under the president's jurisdiction.

In the 1920s the Reserve developed into a force of citizen sailors under federal control. A Reserve unit may be called to active duty in the event of a local or national emergency. Once placed on active duty, a Reserve unit can be assigned anywhere that the Navy decides it is needed, just as an active-duty unit can. Reservists work with regular Navy personnel at sea and onshore in times of war or national emergency. Beginning in 2002 (in the wake of the September 11, 2001, attacks), Navy Reserve units were mobilized for service with American forces in Afghanistan and, later, in Iraq.

During active duty a reservist's salary is made equivalent to that of an active-duty sailor of the same rank. Under federal law a reservist can be kept on active duty no longer than two years. The law also requires the reservist's civilian employer to give a returning reservist his or her former job. The reservist must have notified his or her employer of the call to duty and must return immediately to work.

The Reserve provides trained units that are capable of serving the active-duty Navy with a full range of operations in both peace and war. More than 158,000 men and women serve with the Navy Reserve; about 70,000 of these reservists were actively deployed in 2008.

A reservist is expected to serve a minimum of one weekend a month in drill and work sessions and to participate in

PATHWAYS TO NAVAL SERVICE

The U.S. Navy Reserve responds to natural disasters, such as hurricanes and mudslides. Storekeeper 2nd Class Billy Marcum, a reservist from Kentucky, is part of a search-and-rescue team in Evansville, Indiana, that was called up after an F3 tornado.

two weeks of annual training. A man or woman without previous military service is required to sign up with the Navy Reserve for an eight-year period. Anyone who has already served in the Navy, or in any branch of the military, can enlist for a period of two to six years and then may reenlist with the Reserve for an additional four years.

CAREERS IN THE U.S. NAVY

NAVAL RESERVE OFFICERS TRAINING CORPS

The Naval Reserve Officers Training Corp (NROTC) is the younger brother of Army ROTC. The Army group was founded by Congress in 1862; the Navy followed suit in 1926. The Marine Corps, which functions as a branch of the Navy, joined the program in 1932.

In 1972 the secretary of the Navy authorized sixteen women to enroll in the NROTC program. In 1990 the program was expanded to include students participating in a four-year nursing course; the graduates are granted a commission in the Navy Nurse Corps.

All ROTC programs depend upon the cooperation of participating universities and colleges. As of 2009 colleges and universities in thirty-four states and the District of Columbia offered NROTC programs.

NROTC programs differ little in essentials from place to place. The program has three basic requirements: to wear the ROTC uniform once a week, to participate in unit drill instruction at least once a week, and to attend a naval service course each semester. Otherwise NROTC students live much as their fellow students do.

In addition, the NROTC cadet must complete a regular college course load for a bachelor's degree; studies must include calculus, calculus-based physics, English grammar and composition, and a course in national security policy and American military affairs.

PATHWAYS TO NAVAL SERVICE

NROTC midshipmen from across the country participated in the Career Orientation and Training for Midshipmen (CORTRAMID) aboard the USS *Alaska* in 2006. Midshipman 3rd Class Bryne Welden got a chance to steer the bow of the *Ohio*-class submarine.

The NROTC program offers scholarships to assist its students. The scholarships, which are awarded based on merit and not need, provide full tuition, funds for textbooks and uniforms, and a stipend. They are granted for two- and four-year terms.

A cadet is commissioned after completing his or her NROTC studies; the new officer is obligated to complete

CAREERS IN THE U.S. NAVY

eight years of military service—four years on active duty and four years on Reserve duty, after which he or she may make a career as an officer with the U.S. Navy or the Marine Corps, or become a member of a Reserve unit. ROTC programs produce 60 percent of all officers in the armed forces.

U.S. NAVAL ACADEMY

The U.S. Naval Academy (USNA) in Annapolis, Maryland, was founded in 1845 by the secretary of the Navy as the Naval School. It opened its doors to fifty-six male students and seven professors on October 10. Prior to its founding, young officers had been trained aboard their ships by teachers and fellow officers.

The school was renamed the U.S. Naval Academy in 1850. Students were called naval cadets until 1902, when the name was changed to midshipmen. Midshipmen are junior officers who rank below warrant officers and above master petty officers. About 4,600 men and women attend the USNA annually; women were admitted in 1976 and make up over 20 percent of the class of 2011.

The academy trains officers for both the Navy and the Marine Corps. Annapolis graduates are awarded bachelor of science (BS) degrees, which reflect their four years of study in mathematics, science, engineering, the social sciences, and the humanities. Students bound for the Navy are commissioned as ensigns upon graduation; those joining the Marine Corps receive commissions as second lieutenants.

Admittance to the USNA is competitive and prospective

PATHWAYS TO NAVAL SERVICE

At the graduation and commissioning ceremony, USNA midshipmen and women take the oath of office to become either ensigns in the Navy or second lieutenants in the Marine Corps. The ceremony is held each year at the Navy/Marine Corps Memorial Stadium in Annapolis, Maryland.

students need a nomination to be considered for entrance. Applicants must submit letters requesting a nomination to the president or vice president of the United States, a member of congress, or the secretary of the Navy. Like any other university, Annapolis also requires an application, a personal statement, and letters of recommendation.

The government provides money for the student's tuition, supplies, and board and pays him or her a salary equivalent to that of an ensign. After graduation, the new officer must serve on active duty for at least five years.

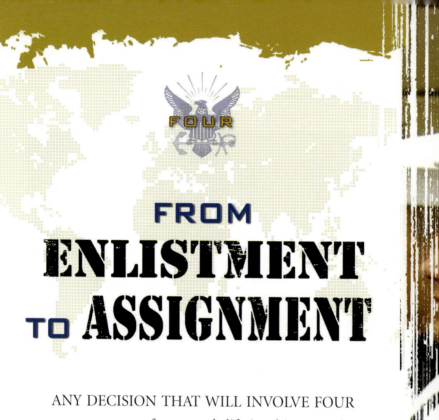

FROM ENLISTMENT TO ASSIGNMENT

ANY DECISION THAT WILL INVOLVE FOUR or more years of a person's life is a big one. The decision to join the Navy is no exception. Some who choose to join are looking for a career, while others want to acquire skills for later civilian use, want to earn the money for college, or simply want to do something that promises adventure and excitement. It can be helpful to talk with family, friends, and even a favorite teacher before making a final decision. Whatever the motive for joining, the first step is enlisting.

ENLISTMENT

Enlistment begins at a local Navy recruiting station, where a recruiter will provide an introduction to

Sailors stand in formation at the U.S. Navy Memorial in Washington, DC, where the statue of the Lone Sailor is located. Some new recruits are selected to be members of the U.S. Navy Ceremonial Guard and are trained to perform military ceremonial honors.

life in the Navy and answer a prospective enlistee's questions. Once the final decision is made, the enlistee needs to bring a number of documents to the recruiter for review:

1. Birth certificate
2. Social security card
3. High school diploma and, if applicable, college transcript
4. A list of jobs held and places worked since age sixteen
5. Contact information for four personal references
6. A list of problems with the police, if any, including minor traffic violations
7. A list of places visited outside the United States
8. A list of places lived since age sixteen
9. A medical history, including a list of current medications

Noncitizens need to bring their permanent resident (green card) number and port of entry place and date.

After the information has been reviewed and discussed with the enlistee, the recruiter will fill out a preliminary medical report that will be reviewed by a doctor. Once approved, the enlistee is sent to a local military entrance processing station (MEPS), where he or she undergoes a complete physical examination (including hearing and vision testing, blood and urinalysis, and a pregnancy test for women, and takes the Armed Services Vocational Aptitude Battery (ASVAB).

The ASVAB consists of a series of multiple-choice tests. It is not an intelligence (IQ) or academic test; its main purpose is to target the career best suited for the

FROM ENLISTMENT TO ASSIGNMENT

enlistee based on his or her interests and abilities. The ASVAB tests seek to determine aptitude in several areas: general science, arithmetic reasoning, electronics, and mechanical comprehension.

After the medical examination and the vocational testing are completed, the enlistee is interviewed by a career classifier, who will advise the enlistee on career possibilities and review his or her background. Finally, with a counselor present, the enlistee will review and sign the enlistment contract.

Upon completion of these steps comes the oath of enlistment ceremony. Enlistees stand before a commissioned officer and recite the oath that makes them members of the U.S. Navy:

> I, _____, do solemnly swear (or affirm) that I will support and defend the Constitution of the United States against all enemies, foreign and domestic; that I will bear true faith and allegiance to the same; and that I will obey the orders of the President of the United States and the orders of the officers appointed over me, according to regulations and the Uniform Code of Military Justice. So help me God.

Not everyone who has taken the oath of enlistment proceeds immediately to boot camp; some take advantage of the Navy's Delayed Entry Program (DEP), which allows an enlistee to wait as long as a year before reporting for

CAREERS IN THE U.S. NAVY

At the end of their first year at the USNA, midshipmen must compete in the day-long Sea Trials, which consists of obstacle courses, long-distance runs, and damage-control situations. The trials are meant to test the midshipmen both physically and mentally.

FROM ENLISTMENT TO ASSIGNMENT

duty. After the enlistment ceremony, people in the program return to school; work; or family, business, or personal matters. Even though their lives as civilians continues, they are still in the Navy and must report for duty at the agreed upon time.

BOOT CAMP

From the enlistment station, enlistees are sent to Recruit Training Command (RTC) at Great Lakes Naval Training Center, in Waukegan, Illinois, for a period of basic instruction, better known in the navy as boot camp. Each year 50,000 men and women attend boot camp.

All new recruits are formed into divisions and placed under a recruit division commander (RDC), who is a petty officer or chief petty officer. RDCs are men and women who have been selected for their teaching skills and leadership abilities. The RDC will guide his or her division through boot camp and help to hone the new recruits' basic naval skills.

A recruit division is made up of approximately eighty men and women. They dorm in buildings known as "ships," which house a thousand people, and are responsible for keeping their quarters up to stringent Navy standards of neatness and cleanliness. Though the men and women train together, they are housed separately.

Boot camp lasts for eight weeks and is divided into two types of instruction: classroom and field training. Recruits must pass exams in both to graduate from boot camp.

CAREERS IN THE U.S. NAVY

Cryptologic Technician Technical Seaman Apprentice Ashley Wise learns to fire a handgun with the help of Aviation Ordanceman 3rd Class Ricky Spooner aboard the USS *Wasp*. Weapons training will qualify Wise to stand watch.

CLASSROOM TRAINING

An enlistee's classroom training begins with learning the insignia that identify the various officer and enlisted ranks. Instruction continues with the following subjects:
- The chain of command
- Military customs and courtesies
- Core navy values. The emphasis is on establishing the traditions of honor, courage, and commitment.
- Drilling and marching. These skills are necessary to

FROM ENLISTMENT TO ASSIGNMENT

enable a military force—no matter its size or the problems facing it—to act with the speed and efficiency of a single person.
- Conduct during armed conflict
- Ship and aircraft identification
- Career advancement

FIELD TRAINING

Field training includes swimming, first-aid instruction, and becoming familiar with weapons. Navy recruits also learn basic shipboard tasks while at boot camp:
- Standing watch
- Semaphore (signaling with flags)
- Extinguishing fires
- Carrying and using fire hoses
- Opening and closing watertight doors
- Escaping smoke-filled compartments
- Operating the oxygen breathing apparatus
- Mastering the Confidence Chamber

The purpose of Confidence Chamber training is to instill discipline and confidence in the trainees so that they can respond to a frightening situation calmly and rationally. About one hundred trainees put on gas masks and go into the Confidence Chamber, where tear gas is released. The instructor orders the trainees to remove their gas masks and recite their names and social security numbers before allowing them to exit the chamber.

CAREERS IN THE U.S. NAVY

THE FINAL HURDLE

The culmination of boot camp training comes in the seventh week with a day-long challenge called Battle Stations. It requires all recruits to demonstrate their proficiency in the various areas they have studied. The eighth week is the final week of boot camp. It closes with a graduation ceremony, a full-dress affair to which family and friends may be invited. Graduation marks the end of training and the beginning of life as an active-duty sailor.

Navy training operations are often demanding, but they prepare sailors for missions in all conditions. These sailors wade from their craft toward the shore while carrying full supply packs on their backs.

FROM ENLISTMENT TO ASSIGNMENT

ON-DUTY TRAINING

The Navy offers courses for career sailors to enhance their job skills and to stay up-to-date in general military matters. After boot camp sailors begin training in a specific field at an "A" school or in apprenticeship training, or they are assigned to general training.

A new enlistee who showed a talent for a certain field on the ASVAB may be assigned to train in that field at one of the Navy's specialty training centers, called A schools. The length of time spent in A school depends on the sailor's career choice. After completion, a sailor is either assigned to a duty station or sent to another school for additional training.

Many new sailors are assigned to apprenticeship training programs, which combine classroom and on-the-job training. There are programs available in over 120 trades, and sailors are assigned based on their ASVAB results. Depending on the field, a sailor will spend between twelve and eighteen months in further training at a Navy station.

A recruit who has not decided on a career at the end of boot camp may be assigned to general training in various fields, after which he or she will serve a term of apprenticeship in the fleet.

ENLISTED RANKS

Few things in the life of a sailor have more daily impact than rank, and rank is directly linked to pay. A rank is a title, and a pay grade, or level, is an alphanumeric designation. The

CAREERS IN THE U.S. NAVY

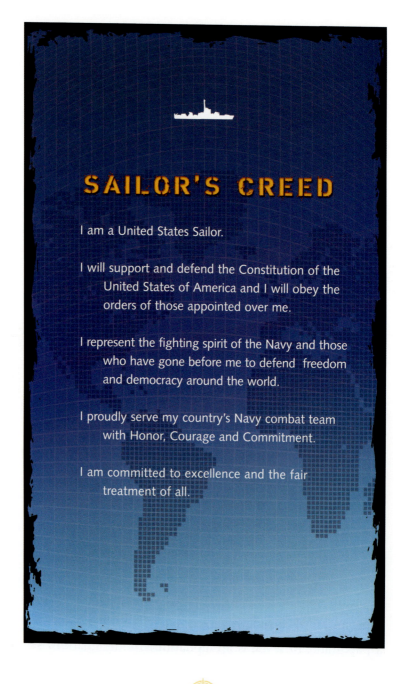

SAILOR'S CREED

I am a United States Sailor.

I will support and defend the Constitution of the United States of America and I will obey the orders of those appointed over me.

I represent the fighting spirit of the Navy and those who have gone before me to defend freedom and democracy around the world.

I proudly serve my country's Navy combat team with Honor, Courage and Commitment.

I am committed to excellence and the fair treatment of all.

FROM ENLISTMENT TO ASSIGNMENT

LCDR Jennifer Tredway is promoted while aboard the USNS *Comfort*, a military sealift command hospital. CAPT Craig Shepherd and CAPT Bruce Boynton pin new epaulettes on Tredway, a surgical nurse. All three officers are with the U.S. Public Health Service (PHS).

nine Navy pay grades for enlisted personnel begin with the letter E.

The ranks of Seaman Recruit, Seaman Apprentice, and Seaman are pay grades E-1 through E-3, respectively. Once being promoted to Petty Officer 3rd Class (E-4), a sailor is considered a noncommissioned officer (NCO) and assumes leadership duties and responsibilities. NCOs are enlisted soldiers who have shown themselves to have command capabilities. A commissioned officer usually has at least a college degree and has undergone special training; he or she

NAVY RANK INSIGNIA

ENLISTED RANKS

Badges on a sailor's uniform indicate his or her rank (pay grade) and, for petty officer third class and above, his or her rating (job). Insignia are silver on blue uniforms and navy blue on white uniforms. Rating insignia are located between the chevrons and the eagle. Below are the rank insignia for all Navy enlisted personnel.

- Seaman Recruit (SR): no rank insignia
- Seaman Apprentice (SA)
- Seaman (SN)
- Petty Officer Third Class (PO3)
- Petty Officer Second Class (PO2)
- Petty Officer First Class (PO1)
- Chief Petty Officer (CPO)
- Senior Chief Petty Officer (SCPO)
- Master Chief Petty Officer (MCPO)
- Force or Fleet Command Master Chief Petty Officer (FORMC or FLTMC)
- Master Chief Petty Officer of the Navy (MCPON)

OFFICERS

Commissioned officers display their rank and rating insignia on the collar, the shoulder, or the lower sleeve depending on what uniform they are wearing. Below are the rank insignia for all naval officers.

 Ensign (ENS)

 Rear Admiral Upper Half (RADM)(U)

 Lieutenant Junior Grade (LTJG)

 Vice Admiral (VADM)

 Lieutenant (LT)

 Admiral (ADM)

 Lieutenant Commander (LCDR)

 Fleet Admiral (FADM)

 Commander (CDR)

 Chief Warrant Officer 2 (CWO2)

 Chief Warrant Officer 3 (CWO3)

 Captain (CAPT)

 Chief Warrant Officer 4 (CWO4)

 Rear Admiral Lower Half (RADM)(L)

CAREERS IN THE U.S. NAVY

delegates responsibility to NCOs. Petty Officers 3rd Class, 2nd Class (E-5), and 1st Class (E-6) are rated. This means that they have an occupational specialty.

The final three pay grades include the highest-ranking NCOs: Chief Petty Officer (E-7), Senior Chief Petty Officer (E-8), and Master Chief Petty Officer (E-9). To become senior NCOs, sailors must have acquired great technical expertise in their field, be able to handle extensive administrative duties, and provide leadership and support to the men and women beneath them.

The importance of senior NCOs to the Navy is indicated by the fact that they wear distinctive uniforms and have separate berthing and dining facilities. A sailor promoted to chief petty officer participates in a formal ceremony that is attended by the other petty officers.

Within pay grade E-9 the highest rank is Master Chief Petty Officer of the Navy. Very few enlisted personnel ever achieve this rank; those who do serve as special assistants to the highest-ranking commissioned officers in all matters pertaining to the enlisted personnel within their commands. Only one Master Chief Petty Officer of the Navy serves at a time and he or she reports directly to the chief of naval operations, the Navy's highest-ranking officer.

NAVAL OFFICERS

Any active or Reserve sailor or Marine who wishes to become an officer may apply for admission to the Navy's

FROM ENLISTMENT TO ASSIGNMENT

Officer Candidate School (OCS) in Pensacola, Florida, which trains men and women to serve as officers in either the Navy or the Marine Corps. All men and women with a bachelor's degree or higher from an accredited college or university are eligible for acceptance.

The thirteen-week course incorporates both academic and physical training. The academic training includes work and study in navigation, seamanship, damage control, and naval leadership. The physical instruction involves a regular regimen of calisthenics, running, and aquatics.

On successfully completing the course, the new officer may choose to be commissioned as an ensign with the Navy or a second lieutenant with the Marine Corps. Commissioned naval officers are classified into ten pay grades, designated by the letter O, and eleven ranks.

Warrent officers are highly trained experts in a specific field. They are given warrants from the secretary of the Navy and receive presidential commissions. The five pay grades are designated by the letter W.

SALARY AND BENEFITS

THERE ARE FINANCIAL, EDUCATIONAL, AND personal benefits available to members of the U.S. Navy. The benefits for full-time active-duty sailors and reservists differ somewhat.

BENEFITS

ENLISTED REGULAR

1. Full-time salary
2. Thirty days paid vacation annually
3. Retirement income plus savings program
4. Free medical, dental, and hospital care (includes family members, if married)
5. Low-cost post exchange (PX) (department store) and commissary (grocery store) privileges
6. Low-cost life insurance policies

The USS *Harry S. Truman*, transporting Carrier Air Wing 3, receives supplies from the USNS *Arctic*, a military sealift command fast combat support ship (rear), in the Persian Gulf.

CAREERS IN THE U.S. NAVY

7. Extra income includes allowances for subsistence housing and uniforms

RESERVE

1. Part-time salary
2. Full-time pay and allowance for meals and housing during the two-week annual training period
3. Health care for injury or illness during active duty or training periods
4. Low-cost life insurance
5. PX and commissary privileges
6. Retirement income or pay

SALARY AND SPECIAL PAY

Pay for all members of the U.S. Navy, enlisted personnel as well as officers, increases with each rank or grade promotion. Promotion in the lower enlisted grades is normally swift. Promotion to E-2 (Seaman Apprentice) usually takes about nine months; it may then take another nine months to reach E-3 and six more to reach E-4. Salaries also reflect increases in the cost of living allowance (COLA).

In addition to the base salary, compensation is given for work that requires extra duty, greater responsibilities, or hazardous working conditions. Certain highly selective units within the Navy—SEALs, parachutists, divers, and demolition experts—receive extra pay. A sailor is also paid for service in areas where the living conditions are below those at U.S. bases.

SALARY AND BENEFITS

Aviation Warfare Technician 3rd Class Cory Lawrence is one of only a few women who have successfully complete the Navy's Rescue Swimmer School, a physically demanding program that trains enlisted aircrew personnel to rescue and recover aviators and sailors. The course is conducted aboard the Naval Air Station (NAS) in Pensacola, Florida.

CAREERS IN THE U.S. NAVY

EDUCATION

The Navy has always aimed to provide its sailors with the facilities and financial means to improve their lives and careers by continuing their education. Courses for all Navy personnel are available at colleges near duty stations, as correspondence or online courses for those serving in isolated duty stations, and in classrooms aboard ships at sea. The Navy, along with the other military branches, offers programs to sailors seeking financial aid and career assistance.

THE MONTGOMERY GI BILL AND THE NAVY COLLEGE FUND

The Montgomery GI Bill (MGIB) and the Navy College Fund (NCF) are generously endowed government programs that help navy personnel attain their education goals.

Sailors on active duty, as well as certain members of the Navy Reserve, are eligible to apply for these programs, which are intended to finance a college education. As of 2009, a full-time sailor was eligible for approximately $36,000 from the MGIB and $34,000 from the NCF. The money can be used during or after active duty. To qualify, sailors must contribute $100 each month to the Montgomery program during his or her first year of service.

Reservists who want to take advantage of the Montgomery Bill must sign on for six years and maintain a record of satisfactory drill attendance; they are eligible for up to thirty-six months of educational assistance.

SALARY AND BENEFITS

Aviation Electronics Technician 1st Class Megan Reiger looks up at Chief of Naval Operations (CNO) ADM Vern Clark as he reviews her work. Reiger is training at the Naval Aviation Technical Training Center (NATTC), the military's largest training schoolhouse, in Pensacola, Florida.

A CAREER IN NURSING

The Navy Nurse Candidate Program is a program for students who are preparing for careers in nursing and are enrolled full-time (or accepted for enrollment) in an accredited university program. Once accepted into the program, the student becomes an officer candidate (only officers can be Navy nurses) with the Navy Reserve. When a student has successfully

CAREERS IN THE U.S. NAVY

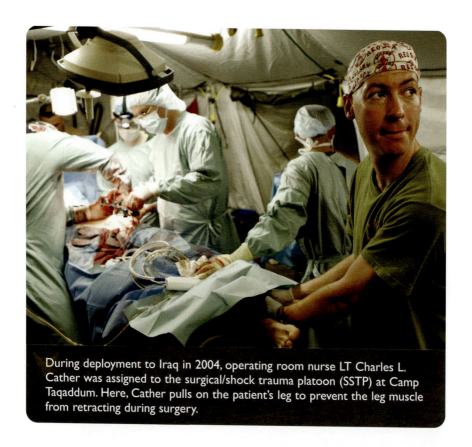

During deployment to Iraq in 2004, operating room nurse LT Charles L. Cather was assigned to the surgical/shock trauma platoon (SSTP) at Camp Taqaddum. Here, Cather pulls on the patient's leg to prevent the leg muscle from retracting during surgery.

completed a nursing degree, he or she is appointed as an ensign in the Nurse Corps of the U.S. Naval Reserve.

To qualify, the applicant must have completed a second year of nursing studies and have more than six months of study left before graduation. Once the course of study is completed, the graduate is required to serve on active duty for five years if he or she entered the program in the third year, and four years if it was the fourth year.

Navy nurses receive tuition assistance and are paid an

SALARY AND BENEFITS

initial $10,000 grant plus a monthly stipend for up to twenty-four months.

NROTC SCHOLARSHIPS

NROTC offers four- and two-year scholarships to college students planning on naval service after graduation.

The scholarships pay for tuition and educational fees (including textbooks) and also provide uniforms and a stipend. The Navy also arranges for recipients of the four-year scholarship to cruise on a naval ship during their summers.

The scholarship program has strict requirements. Good grades, consistent class attendance, high class ranking, good college entrance exam results, and extracurricular activities are important factors.

As with all NROTC cadets, scholarship recipients are commissioned as officers at graduation and must fulfill an eight-year service obligation.

ACCELERATE YOUR LIFE

Service in the U.S. Navy or the Navy Reserve are equally admirable and can provide great opportunities and lead to a satisfying career. Information on service in the U.S. Army, the Air Force, the Marine Corps, and the Coast Guard is available in the other books in this series, which explain how each branch provides job opportunities, adventure, and experience in a wide variety of activities and fields.

ACRONYM GLOSSARY

ASVAB	Armed Services Vocational Aptitude Battery
ASW	Anti-submarine warfare
BCT	Basic combat training
BNCOC	Basic Noncommissioned Officer Course
CIC	Combat information center
CNO	Chief of Naval Operations
COLA	Cost of living allowance
CORTRAMID	Career orientation and training for midshipmen
DEP	Delayed entry program
E	Enlisted, in pay grade designation
EOD	Explosive ordnance disposal technician
IFF	Identification Friend or Foe, a surveillance system
MEPS	Military Entrance Processing Station
MGIB	Montgomery GI Bill
MMA	Multimission maritime aircraft
NAS	Naval air station
NATTC	Naval Aviation Technical Training Center
NCF	Navy College Fund
NCO	Noncommissioned officer
NROTC	Naval Reserve Officers Training Corps
O	Officer, in pay grade designation
OCS	Officer Candidate School
PHS	Public Health Service
PX	Post exchange; also called base exchange (BX)
RDC	Recruit division commander
ROTC	Reserve Officers Training Corps
RTC	Recruit training command
SEAL	Sea, air, land
SOF	Special Operations Forces
SSTP	Surgical/shock trauma platoon
STOVL	Short takeoff/vertical landing

SWCC	Special warfare combatant-craft crewman
USNA	United States Naval Academy
USS	United States ship
USNS	United States naval ship
VLS	Vertical launch system
V/STOL	Vertical/short takeoff and landing
VTOL	Vertical takeoff and landing
W	Warrant officer, in pay grade designation
WAVES	Women Accepted for Volunteer Emergency Service

FURTHER INFORMATION

WEBSITES

The official website of the U.S. Navy
www.navy.mil

The website of the U.S. Navy Reserve
www.navyreserve.com

The website of the U.S. Navy for new and potential recruits
www.navy.com

The website of the NROTC program
www.nrotc.navy.mil

The website of the U.S. Naval Academy
www.usna.edu

SELECTED BIBLIOGRAPHY

Axelrod, Alan, and Charles Phillips. *Macmillan Dictionary of Military Biography*. New York: Macmillan, 1998.

Chambers, John Whiteclay, II, ed. *Oxford Companion to American Military History*. New York: Oxford University Press, 1999.

Holmes, Richard, ed. *Oxford Companion to Military History*. New York: Oxford University Press, 2001.

U.S. Navy. Fact File. http://www.navy.mil/navydata/fact.asp (accessed July 29, 2008).

INDEX

Page numbers in **boldface** are illustrations, tables, and charts.

active-duty Navy, 42, 44
administration, 32
aircraft, 26–27
aircraft carriers, 14–16, **17**
Alaska, USS, **49**
American Revolution, 7–8
amphibious assault ships, **17**, 18–19
Arctic, USNS, **69**
Arleigh Burke class, 20
Arleigh Burke–class destroyer, 7
Armed Services Vocational Aptitude Battery (ASVAB), 54–55
attack submarines, 24–25
aviation, 32–33

ballistic missile submarines, 23–24
Barbary Pirates, 9
bases, naval, 28–29
Battle Stations, 60
benefits, 68–70
Bonhomme Richard, 21
boot camp, 44, **45**, 57–60
Boynton, Bruce, **63**

Carrier Air Wing 1, **13**
Carrier Air Wing 3, **69**
Cather, Charles L., **74**
civilian ships, 8
Clark, Vern, **73**
classroom training, 58–59
combat forces
 submarine, 23–25
 surface, 12–22
Comfort, USNS, 63
communications and intelligence, 35, 43

Confidence Chamber, 59
construction and building, 33–34
Continental Congress, 7–9
Countess of Scarborough, 21
Critchfield, Kearah, **43**
cruisers, 19–20

Delayed Entry Program (DEP), 55
destroyers, 20
early-warning aircraft, 26–27
education, 34, 72–75
electronics and computers, 34
emergency, fire and rescue, 34–35
enlisted ranks, 61, 63–66
enlistment, 52, 54–55, 57
Enterprise class, 15–16

field training, 59
fighter or attack aircraft, 26, **27**
Fighting Seabees, 35–36, **36**
flag signals (semaphore), 43
flashing light, 43
fleets, 27–28
food, restaurant and lodging, 35
frigates, 9, 20, 22

Gator Navy, 18–19
George H. W. Bush, USS, 16
Gerald R. Ford class, 16
GI Bill, 72
Gordon, Ladonna, **38**
G-suit, 27, **27**
Guantánamo Bay, Cuba, 29

Harpers Ferry, USS, **43**
Harry S. Truman, USS, **33**, **69**
helicopters, **10**, 19, 27
Hornet, 26, **27**
human resources, 37, 40

insignia, naval rank, 64–65
intelligence and communications, 35, 43

job selection and variety, 9, 30–37, 40–41
Jones, John Paul, 21, **21**

Kings Bay, Georgia, 29
Kitsap, Washington, 29
Kitty Hawk class, 15

law enforcement, 34–35
Lawrence, Cory, **71**
letters of marque, 8
Los Angeles class, **22–23**, 24–25

Marcum, Billy, **47**
mechanical and industrial, 35–36
media and public affairs, 36–37
medical and dental, 37
Montgomery GI Bill, 72
Montpelier, USS, **22–23**
MV-22 Osprey, **17**

naval air forces, 26–27
Naval Aviation Technical Training Center (NATTC), **73**
Naval Militia, 45–47
naval officers, 66–67
Naval Reserve Officers Training Corps (NROTC), 42, 48–50, 75
Naval School, 50
Navy College Fund (NCF), 72
Navy Nurse Candidate Program, 73–75
Navy Nurse Corps, 48
Navy Week, 38–39
Nimitz class, 16

Norfolk, Virginia, 28

oath of enlistment, 55
Officer Candidate School (OCS), 66–67
Ohio class, 23–24, **49**
O'Kane, USS, 7
Oliver Hazard Perry class, 22
on-duty training, 61

patrol aircraft, 26
Pearl Harbor, Hawaii, 28–29
Pensacola, Florida, 29
Pentagon, 29
pirates, 9
Pomeroy, William, **31**

ranks, enlisted, 61, 63–66
ratings, 32–41
Reiger, Megan, **73**
religion, 37, 40
requirements
    to join U.S. Navy, 42, 44
    for U.S. Naval Academy, 50–51
Rescue Swimmer School, 71
Revolutionary War, 7–8

Sailor's Creed, 62
salary and benefits, 68–75
San Diego, California, 28
scholarships, 49, 75
Seabees, 35–36, **36**
Sea Stallion helicopters, **10**
Sea Trials, 56, **56**
Seawolf class, 25
security, 34–35
semaphore (flag signals), 43
Serapis, 21
Shepherd, Craig, **63**

ships
   submarine, 23–25
   surface forces, 12–22
   USS/USNS designations, 14
special operations forces (SOF), 40, **41**
special pay and salary, 70
Spooner, Ricky, **58**
submarine forces, combat, 23–25
support services, 27–29
surface forces, combat, 12–22

Tarawa class, 18–19
Theodore Roosevelt, USS, **10–11**, **13**
Ticonderoga, USS, 20
Ticonderoga class, 19–20
transport aircraft, 26
transportation and logistics, 40–41
Tredway, Jennifer, **63**

U.S. Army, 8

U.S. Naval Academy, 42, 50–51
U.S. Naval Submarine School, 25
U.S. Navy Ceremonial Guard, **53**
U.S. Navy Reserve, 42, 45–47

Vella Gulf, USS, **31**
Virginia class, 25

warships, 8, 9
Wasp, USS, **17**, **58**
Wasp class, 18
Welden, Bryne, **49**
Wijnaldum, Kathryn S., **38**
Wise, Ashley, **58**
women
   in the Navy, 38–39, 48
   U.S. Naval Academy, 50
World War I, 38–39
World War II, 38–39

Yokosuko, Japan, 29

ABOUT THE AUTHOR

EDWARD F. DOLAN is the author of more than 120 published nonfiction books. His most recent book for Marshall Cavendish Benchmark is *George Washington* in the series Presidents and Their Times. Mr. Dolan is a California native and currently resides near San Francisco.